BUILDING YOU

HOW TO *REALLY* SUCCEED IN
NETWORK MARKETING

MICHAEL B. ROSS

WITH
DAVID M. BAKER

Mainstream Life Solutions, LLC
15381 Pugh Road, #4
East Liverpool, Ohio 43920

Printed in the United States of America

Book design and edited by Brittany M. Ross

TABLE OF CONTENTS

ACKNOWLEDGMENTS

Without the continued help and support of my gorgeous, thoughtful and talented wife Brittany Ross, this book would not have been possible.

Also, I would like to thank Roberta Baker for supporting her husband Dave, during long days and late nights.

Last, but certainly not least we would like to thank the core of our team. Dr. Ben and Mary Jo Mrozek, John Tindell, Ellen Mcghee, Mike Holtom, Laura Allshouse, Laura Van Dyne, Don Keck, Mark Cole, Kevin Ours, Mike Sodomora, Zachary Dorn, Jason Hicks, Ray Ganancial, Bob and Ronda Tatgenhorst, Chris Brock and many more.

We love you guys. This book was written for you.

FOREWARD

Have you ever wondered why some people succeed in just about everything and others find failure at every turn? Don't let this bother you. If you entered into direct selling company, the industry standards of success will astonish you. One in one hundred succeed. Yet the industry continues to grow each year. In some circles the goal is to bring in as many new recruits as possible and let the chips fall where they may. "Go, go, go, you're a rock star, get them in, sign them up and move on." Sound familiar? This is also the main reason people fail and the industry as a whole has such a bad name.

In fact, if you check with people around you, I bet you will hear horror stories about almost every direct selling company. "It's a scam, it's a pyramid scheme, it's one of those get rich quick things." The direct selling industry has done very little to stop it. Why should they. If billions of dollars can be made with only one in one hundred succeeding, why fix it? When Michael and I began the process of writing this book we were also in the process of building a successful network within a particular direct selling company.

Within the first year, we had built our company with 100 plus in our down line and were closing in on our 10k a month goal. Then something happened. When we turned to look behind us we found something disheartening—only a few people were succeeding and no one was having the level of success we were having. How could this be? We had meetings, trainings, seminars to motivate and empower our rep's, yet only a handful were seeing success. This did not sit very well with us. Our desire was to see every person on our team succeed.

What we did next surprised everyone. We stopped. We had achieved a status within the company and were only a few short months away from the upper echelon. We dropped everything. We were not willing to accept the one in one hundred success rate. We were not willing to make hundreds of thousands of dollars off the backs of people who joined our team. How could we promote success to everyone knowing full well that their chances to succeed were minimal at best? The people that were signing up wanted—and most of the time— needed to succeed. They joined our team because our meetings and seminars promoted success at every turn. "Anyone can do it. It's so easy, all you have to do is sign up and you can make it." Simply not true.

In December of 2010 Mainstream Life Solutions, LLC was founded. Our goal with our company is to provide the tools to help people succeed, not only in direct selling, but in relationships as well. Our team has devoted countless hours in developing this system. We hope after reading this book, you will meet success face-to-face in this industry and every facet of life.

May God Bless you in your journey

David M. Baker
Co-Founder, Mainstream Life Solutions

INTRODUCTION

Building a business takes effort. The network marketing or direct selling industry takes real business wherewithal, focus, acumen, desire, faith, courage, and commitment. If you are not willing to put the proper time into building your business, please don't waste your time reading. Return your representative information to its proper place and go back to your life.

To the brave souls who continue reading: Congratulations! You've made a decision to become a better person. Where you are in life— at the top or at the bottom— it doesn't matter. You are about to learn things that can't be learned in any other industry with the same authenticity.

Be implored from the following passage of scripture:

Be doers of the word, and not hearers only, deceiving yourselves.
For if anyone is a hearer of the word and not a doer, he is like a man
who observes his natural face in a mirror; for he observes himself
and goes away and at once forgets what he was like. But he who
looks into the perfect law, the law of liberty, and perseveres, being
no hearer that forgets but a doer that acts, he shall be blessed in his
doing. (James 1:22-25)

It's the action that counts. Anyone can succeed in this industry; but it takes work. Just like anyone can succeed, anyone can fail. The choice is yours alone.

You entered the direct selling industry with wallet in hand and dreams of a brighter financial future in heart. You believed enough in the company you represent to make a minimal financial investment, hoping to achieve your dreams. At that moment, a different financial future was within reach. You thought to yourself: I can do this. But what will happen when you experience your first rejection, someone blows off an appointment, or acts cynically about your new business? Will you allow it to push those dreams of a bright financial future out of reach?

If this industry were effortless, everyone would be a millionaire. It's not "get rich quick," it's "get rich slow." Those who persevere will see great success. Commitment to this business must be long-term. This book will teach you how to:

- Determine your "Why" - Knowing why you started your business will allow you to keep the long-term in perspective.

- Develop daily, weekly and monthly goals – Set goals and take steps to reach them.

- Effectively dedicate time to your business – You must treat your business like a business. If you invest nothing into your business, you can expect an equal return.

- Think and be positive - No one wants to be around a negative person, let alone partner with them in business.

- Be sincere - The sincerity and belief you have in your company will speak volumes to your prospects.

- Be other-minded - Help others see how joining your team could change their lives. Don't be focused solely on your dreams and vision.

- Be a strategic communicator - Good communicators make a complicated subject simple.

CHAPTER 1

BUILDING A FOUNDATION

Education is the foundation upon which we build our future.
Christine Gregoire

WHAT IS DIRECT SELLING?

Direct selling, commonly referred to as network marketing, is a method of product and service distribution that involves an estimated 59-million people worldwide. The Direct Selling Association defines direct selling as "the sale of a consumer product or service, person-to-person, away from a fixed retail location, marketed through independent sales representatives."

Customers can purchase products or services from most any industry through direct selling companies. Beauty products, jewelry, phone services, nutritional supplements, internet and television services are all promoted through direct selling companies.

Companies using the direct selling method capitalize on "relationship marketing." Relationship marketing is the marketing of products or services by one individual to another based on an existing relationship. Everyone, regardless of their "official" involvement in direct selling, participates in relationship marketing. Think about it: What do you do when you see a great movie, eat at an awesome restaurant or receive exceptional customer service while having your car repaired? The natural response is to share that experience with people in your life. You influence them to check out that movie, go to that restaurant or take their car to that shop. Based on your referral, your friends and family do business with the places you've recommended.

So it goes with direct selling: You recommend the products or services you represent to the people in your life.

Relationship marketing benefits both the companies that employ it and the customers gathered through it by fostering a customer-centric approach. Customers will be more loyal to the companies you represent because of their personal relationship with you. Customers will receive optimal care because you, someone who's invested in them personally, providing that care.

A term often associated with direct selling is multi-level marketing (MLM). MLM is not a type of company or industry; it is a type of compensation plan found in the direct selling industry. Instead of using a single-level compensation plan, many direct selling companies utilize a MLM compensation plan.

Compensation is based on an independent representative's (IR) product and service sales, and the sales made by an IR's downline. This encourages IRs of direct selling companies to build a business while still placing an emphasis on product and service sales.

Within the direct selling industry, the terms "downline" and "upline" are used to describe where an IR falls within the multiple levels of a direct selling company. A downline is comprised of people an IR has enrolled into their business, as well as the IRs those people sponsor. An upline is comprised of the IRs whom you are enrolled under. This includes your sponsor. In a well-structured direct selling company, the earning potential of an IR should not be dictated by who enrolled that IR or where that person falls in an upline or downline. In a solid direct selling company, IR's who outperform those in their upline should have the ability to earn more than their upline. With focus on personal sales efforts, growth, hard work and self-discipline IR's should have the ability to achieve more success than that of their sponsor.

UNDERSTANDING THE INDUSTRY

Nobody can excel in something they don't understand. The following section will give you basic understanding of the history, evolvement and the pulse of the direct selling industry. Knowing where direct selling started, where it has been and where it's going will prepare you to build your business successfully.

Have you've heard this objection: "That looks like one of those 'pyramid things'?" This resistance is common. If you've been in direct selling for any length of time, you've noticed the stigma that envelopes the industry. One author put it this way: "In many circles, you might as well declare yourself as being a leper than admit to being in network marketing."

Direct selling provides a significant opportunity for an insignificant investment. It epitomizes capitalism and offers a potential for wealth that its participants couldn't find elsewhere. So how has direct selling industry gotten such a bad rap?

To answer this question, we will begin with the industry's history. In the 1940's California Vitamins (later called Nutralite Food Supplement Corporation) pioneered the direct selling industry when the company found it more lucrative to have a lot of sales representatives selling a few products then to employ a small sales force to sell a lot of products. The company discovered that this new model generated more sales than the traditional sales model. Also, the company noticed that a large portion of its customer base was the friends and families of sales representatives which contributed to customer loyalty.

Existing satisfied customers evolved into new sales representatives and a multi-level commission-based pay plan was established. The commission plan encouraged salespeople to invite their customers to become salespeople themselves. Individuals were then compensated for the sales generated by both themselves and their team. This is where the idea of "downlines" and "uplines" emerged.

Direct selling expanded in 1959 when successful Nutralite distributers Richard DeVos and Jay Van Andel developed Amway— the "American way" of marketing products.

Prior to the emergence of legitimate direct selling companies, pyramid schemes surfaced. Pyramid schemes exchange money for "the right to involve others" without legitimate products or services changing hands. Pyramid schemes are said to be associated with the "chain letter phenomenon," which deceitfully promised great wealth to participants who mailed "a dime or dollar to the person at the bottom" following World War I. As the chain letter phenomenon subsided, pyramid schemes emerged. By the mid 1970's, pyramid schemes were viewed by legislators as the nation's number one consumer fraud.

This is where a widespread suspicion about direct selling companies began to take root: While pyramid schemes ran rampant, network marketing operated without clear standards or regulations. As the lines between the two became blurred, the Federal Trade Commission (FTC) turned their focus to all direct selling companies in order to clean up pyramid schemes.

The industry was brand new, unregulated and misunderstood. In 1975, the FTC filed suit against Amway stating that its refusal to sell its products in retail stores was a "restraint of trade" and alleging that the company was an illegal pyramid. After four years and millions of dollars in legal fees, the FTC ruled that Amway was not an illegal pyramid.

In addition, the FTC acknowledged the legitimacy of network marketing and its legal and efficient distribution system. The favorable outcome for Amway made no difference to people who look at direct selling and assume illegal pyramiding.

However, the ruling in the Amway case brought new regulations to direct selling which helped to legitimize the industry and mark out clear standards by which it should be run. These "retail rules" required that:

- distributers must have 10 customers each month
- distributers must sell, not stockpile, at least 70 percent of goods
- companies must allow for the return of merchandise

Clear regulations and acknowledgment from the FTC caused the industry to explode in the next decade. Today, thousands of network marketing companies operate worldwide and network marketing is said to be a 100 billion dollar industry.

Unfortunately, as in many of life's arenas, first impressions are everything. The emergence of direct selling and the commencement of pyramid scheming was bad timing for the industry. It has caused many people to look at direct selling companies with skepticism and negativity.

Regardless of that stigma, many direct selling companies and independent representatives are achieving great success. With that in mind, the stigma surrounding the industry is just another obstacle to overcome on the journey of reaching your business goals.

Overcoming takes education and understanding. To further explore the stigma behind direct selling, we must look at common criticisms of the industry.

Here are a few reasons why the industries reputation remains less than perfect:

- alleged price-fixing
- cost for joining
- emphasis on recruitment rather than sales
- potential exploitation of relationships

Obviously, direct selling companies should be evaluated on a case-by-case basis. It's unfair to view the entire industry negatively because of a few "bad eggs." Are there direct selling companies that fix prices? Sure. Do some companies require a high investment to join? Absolutely. Are some direct selling companies focused on "recruiting"? Definitely.

But not all direct selling companies operate this way. There are legitimate direct selling companies with great business plans and opportunities. Before joining a direct selling company, it's important to do your research. You must evaluate for yourself if the company you're seeking is a company you're confident representing.

You must ask yourself:

- Do I believe in the way this company operates?
- Do I believe in the opportunity the company provides?
- Do I understand how the company works? If not, does the company provide resources to help me understand?

If you've answered yes to all of these, nothing should stop you from building your direct selling business with that company.

Still, there are other reasons why a stigma looms around the direct selling industry. One important factor is that a huge majority of people who join direct selling companies don't turn a profit. According to the founder of the Consumer Awareness Institute, 99 percent of people who join a network marketing company lose money rather than make money.

Why? Surely the fault is not in industry standards or in each company's business plan. If that were the case, the FTC would put the stop to direct selling altogether. What's the difference between the one percent who makes money and the other 99 percent who loses money?

Perseverance, hard work, training, professionalism, business savvy and credibility are a few traits separating the successful and the unsuccessful. What's the good news? By taking steps to grow as a person and a business owner (by reading this book, for example) you are well on your way to becoming part of that one percent.

Everyone knows someone who committed to something and didn't stick with it. Take New Year's resolutions for example. Among the most popular resolutions is getting physically fit. If you go to a gym in the first week of January, it will be filled to the brim. Check out that same gym at that same time in April and you won't see half of the faces you saw just a few months earlier. Sadly, not a whole lot of people have the "stick-to-it-iveness" it takes to make it in direct selling. When many people experience their first rejection, encounter someone who talks negatively about their business or realize success in the industry takes extra work and effort, they give up, believing that "network marketing never works" or that the company they were a part of was "just a scam."

The fact is there are people who succeed in direct selling. They are people who overcome problems, persevere through trials and constantly educate themselves. Be one of those people and you will go far in your business.

Ultimately, the issues with direct selling generate at the individual level not the industry level.

In an intriguing article titled "The Real Problem with Network Marketing and Multi-Level Marketing" author Scott Allen writes that issues with the industry aren't because of the business model itself. After all, every sales organization follows a pyramid structure and payment for joining is a standard franchising model. Allen said that "the real problem with MLM is... some of the people it attracts."

Because of the low cost of entry and the potential to make a substantial amount of money, network marketing is attractive to people who:

- Have not done well professionally or financially
- Have no knowledge of business ownership
- Have no experience or training in sales
- Have unrealistic expectations about the ease in which they could generate income

Because of those reasons, many network marketers oversell the opportunity, discuss business inappropriately in social circumstances, come across as desperate or are inaccurate when discussing their business.

You may have scanned the above list of bullet points and saw a few that describe you. If so, don't be discouraged. There isn't a factor listed above that cannot be overcame. Haven't done well professionally or financially? Become a professional. Read the books professionals read. Do the things professionals do. Learn how to handle your finances more appropriately. Create a budget.

Have no knowledge of business ownership? Learn about business ownership. From the mouth of the late Jim Rohn, business philosopher and motivational leader, "there isn't a book you couldn't read, there isn't a class you couldn't take." There is a wealth of knowledge available to those who seek it out. You are the only thing that stands in your way.

Make a decision to become a better you and success in business will follow.

CHAPTER 2

BUILDING YOUR KNOWLEDGE OF PRODUCTS AND SERVICES

An investment in knowledge pays the best interest.
Benjamin Franklin

Gathering products or services for your direct selling company is the most important thing you do. If the value of your company does not come from products or services you should get out now (see chapter one). The number one reason people join direct selling companies is for freedom; they want to work from home and make their own schedule.

In order to achieve freedom through this industry you must become a proficient customer gatherer for the products or services provided through your direct selling company. The more customers and customer loyalty you have, the more money you will make. Also, you need to know how the money works and where it comes from so you can effectively explain your business to others.

FIRST THINGS FIRST

Repeat this phrase as many times as possible: "I am a business owner; I am a professional." When you signed up to distribute products and services for your direct selling company, you committed to becoming a professional business owner. What does it mean to be a professional?

Professionals:

- *Find solutions*

  Customers find problems, professionals find solutions. If you have been used to focusing on problems as a customer it's time to make a change. Find solutions to every problem. Be positive and caring with your customers always. This is the way of a professional.

- *Walk the talk*

  Be truthful about your products or services and every other aspect that applies to your business. If you promise something to your customers; deliver. If not, you will see a significant turnover in customers. If you struggle with telling the truth, please plug into character development training at www.mainstreamlifesolutions.com/character-development.

- *Talk the walk*

  Know what you're talking about and be effective at communicating the benefits of your products or services. Too often, company representatives rely on someone else in their organization to do the talking for them. Again, you are the professional; it is your job to communicate to your customers proficiently and professionally

- *Dress the part*

  Jeans are ok! Direct selling is a laid back industry. Many of your customers will be people you are familiar with so you won't be judged by your appearance with them. However, as you meet new people it will become increasingly important for you to dress the part of a professional. Jeans may still be ok, but make sure you don't under dress for events or meetings.

- *Develop excellence*

  Darren Hardy says, "Be extraordinary because ordinary is average." It's easy to do what's expected of you. Make it a habit to do at least one thing above your customers' expectations. Instead of making your customer pick up their order, deliver it. Make an extra phone call ensuring they like their product or service. Hand-write a note thanking them for their order. When you do the unexpected you'll get extraordinary results.

These five points are good starting blocks to becoming a professional business owner. Sticking to these points is simple but it takes consistency. Be consistent in these five areas and see a great harvest in your business over time by sowing the seeds of professionalism.

PRODUCTS

Out of the top ten direct selling companies, nine of them offer nutritional or care products. Learn what the benefits of using your products are and become adept at explaining the benefits to others. Consumers buy value over cost efficiency. If you can show your potential customer the value of your product and they like how it makes them feel, they will buy from you consistently. Features are part of the product; benefits are the ways that those features positively affect consumers. For example, say that a skin cream contains estriol, an element that fights the signs of aging. A feature of the product is that it contains estriol. A benefit of the product is that it helps fight the signs of aging. Learn how to translate the features of your products into benefits.

An obvious way to learn more about your products is to use them. Personal experience is the best way to explain your product to your customer. If you have a supplement product, purchase a few months' worth and take them consistently. Write down examples of the benefits you've experienced. If you are offer a natural drink product that promises vitality and energy, take the product. Be a spokesperson for the product, understand how it works, and experience the benefits and potential drawbacks. Do the same for beauty care products, vitamins, pet products (please don't take those yourself!), cosmetics, etc. Sell out to your products and speak from experience when referring them to others.

Another way to familiarize yourself with your products is to visit the plant where your company's products are manufactured. This will give you a unique advantage when talking to customers. If you owned a clothing store, wouldn't you visit the manufacturing plant periodically to make sure everything was running smoothly and quality assurance was being maintained? You must treat your direct selling company as if you own everything because when it comes to your franchise, you do.

Products have been the lifeblood of direct selling through the years. Your customer base will increase dramatically if you can explain how your product stands out from commercial product lines.

SERVICES

Over the past twenty years direct selling has transitioned from offering one product or service to offering multiple products and services. Even long-standing, product-driven companies have added services to their arsenal, offering customers and IRs a greater selection and advantage.

Services such as cell phones, television, security systems, and prepaid legal are a network marketing professionals dream because these services are being used by over 75% of the market. According to *All Business*, franchises earn over 30% their investment per year (note: costs accumulate debt for a number of years depending on the franchise). Monthly bills, new contracts, and products sales average around 50 thousand dollars to 500 thousand dollars depending on the location of the franchise. This is not pure profit, however, you can see the type of potential you could have depending on the franchise you own.

By joining a network marketing company you essentially have access to many franchising models allowing you to earn residual income on services that are being used by the majority of people worldwide. You have the earning potential of up to millions of dollars per month without overhead. As network marketers, our job is to connect consumers to corporate companies. The following are prevalent network marketing "franchises":

CELL PHONES

Do you know anyone who doesn't have a cell phone? It is more challenging to find a person that doesn't own a cell phone than it is to find someone with one. Many direct selling companies have tied into this market for two reasons:

1) *Cell phones dominate the market.*

In May 2010, ComScore found that over 234 million U.S. Citizens owned a working cell phone. This yields an estimated 183 billion dollars per year in revenue. The telecommunications industry is dominated by cell phones. Cell phone franchises are growing as technology advances and cheaper plan rates evolve.

2) *Cell phones are a lifestyle.*

When you ask someone to sign their cell service through your franchise, you're not asking them to add something to their life. The monthly reoccurring cell phone bill is already factored in to their budget. Your job is to educate them on the customer added value for making the transition from their current franchise to yours.

TELEVISION

Television service, like cell phones, is a part of the average citizens' lifestyle making it a great benefit to network marketing representatives. Many times, educated representatives will be able to show the customer the value in switching to their service once their contract with their current provider is fulfilled. The television service industry generates over 100 billion dollars-per-year revenue in service costs and is heavily saturated by franchises.

SECURITY SYSTEMS OR PREPAID LEGAL

With security systems and prepaid legal it is important to target a specific demographic and to know your facts. You must be able to show your customers the added value of having a security system in their home or small business. Identity theft is the number one white-collar crime in the United States today. Education is the key to selling services that people are not currently using.

ONLINE MALLS

Most network marketing companies now have access to their own online shopping mall. Customers and representatives alike can log onto their shopping mall and earn rewards or cash from their respective company. This is another area of network marketing that makes it a unique business opportunity. When disciplined and proactive, representatives can earn significant amounts of money through their online shopping portal.

ENTERTAINMENT

Some companies have entertainment packages that offer significant discounts to customers, who like to shop, travel, play sports, and watch sporting events, etc. Entertainment packages are best presented to customers by highlighting the top 3-5 benefits of purchasing the package. Make sure you study carefully and research what makes your package the best buy.

COMMUNICATIONS

Communications tools through text messaging, email, video conferencing, video phones, webinar, Web site design, and general media are great services to offer your business clients. The more value you can offer your customers, the better. Globalization allows IRs to sell their products online to people all over their country and in other parts of the world. If your company offers communications tools as a part of its service selection, take advantage as often as possible.

BUSINESS BUILDING TOOLS

Almost every company offers their own business building tools. Whether it is inner organization communications tools or a company Web site, be sure to have the necessary tools to build your business. If your company offers its products and services predominately though a Web site and you don't have a Web site you're hurting your business. Invest in every tool available to increase the revenue of your business.

WHERE THE MONEY COMES FROM IN DIRECT SELLING

Technology is changing the world and traditional advertising isn't grabbing the amount of customers it once did. Television commercials aren't being viewed because DVR enables people to record their shows and fast-forward through commercials. Radio advertisements are being bypassed due to the emergence satellite and Internet radio. Companies are seeking out more effective uses of their advertising budgets and relationship marketing fits the bill. The most proficient and reliable form of advertising is word-of-mouth so companies are happy to affiliate themselves with network marketers.

In any franchise the owner must pay royalties to the company they represent. In turn, they make a profit from selling well-known products or services. In most cases from the day a franchise opens they have customers visit the store. Why? Because the brand it represents is well-established and recognizable. Buying franchises is much easier than starting a company from scratch, building name recognition, and developing franchises of your own. Network marketing companies typically do one of two things: They purchase franchises or set up affiliate codes as authorized retailers for specific products and services.

After the direct selling company sets up their products and services they then offer franchises to individuals for a small franchise cost usually between one-hundred and one-thousand dollars.

When an individual purchases a direct selling franchise they are able to sell products and services for the company they represent. They aren't franchise owners of the products and service. Instead, they own a franchise of the network marketing company and are able to offer the services the network marketing company offers.

For example, if Bill owned a franchise for XYZ company and XYZ company offered ABC vitamin products, Bill would be able to sell ABC vitamins. However, if XYZ decided they did not want to offer ABC vitamins any longer, Bill would no longer be able to sell ABC vitamins. As a franchise owner of your company you move as the company moves.

RESIDUAL INCOME

Most direct selling companies have residual income and bonus income worked into their pay plans.

Residual income is money paid as long as the product or service is being used by the customer. For example, you sell a two-year cell phone plan to your friend Albert. Every month Albert pays his bill you will receive a commission on his bill. If Albert's wife Melinda purchases hair and beauty care products from you as well, you will also receive a commission monthly on the beauty care products as Melinda continues ordering them.

Typically, residual income takes time to grow but residual income could replace your full-time income in two to three years. That is, of course, if you work your business steadily and faithfully.

Commission percentages that make up residual income are anywhere from 1-10% on average. If you sold your friend Tommy a security system and it costs him $39.99 per month and you get 10% of that, you will be making $3.99 per month residual on that sale.

Your goal is to have as many products or services paying you as possible. Some network marketers make fifty dollars per month from five to ten customers and some make over 100-thousand dollars per month from tens of thousands of customers. The beauty of direct selling is you can do as little or as much as you would like.

BONUS MONEY

Bonus money sustains new network marketers as they build their residual income. In fact, many people get started in direct selling because they can make instant cash from sales and franchising. Bonus money can pay enough to replace your income in less than six months if you are determined. Bonus money is a one-time payout for the sale of a product or service. The law prohibits representatives making any money until products or services have been sold. Therefore, when a new representative comes into your organization you will not make bonus money until a sale has been made.

In order to comply, companies have created starter kits to sell to new representatives that can be used for resale or self-consumption. Starter kits do three things: 1) they keep the business legal, 2) they release bonus money and 3) they qualify the new representative. Bonus money pays instantly where residual takes time. In many cases, bonus money pays like residual money once you've built a solid foundation in your organization.

Gathering customers is the most important thing in direct selling. As lucrative as bonus money is, never lose sight of the focus of network marketing: to market within your network the products and services your company offers. You are not a recruiter; you are a franchise owner marketing products for the company you represent. Building your business must be done with a solid customer base. Now that we've established the essentials of gathering customers, let's talk about building your business in direct selling.

CHAPTER 3

BUSINESS BUILDING

Education is all a matter of building bridges.

Ralph Ellison

BE THE LEADER YOU WOULD FOLLOW

"Know yourself" is the consistent message Socrates gave his students. He was adamant that knowing yourself was the key to growth. Jim Rohn parroted this notion by saying "Be honest with yourself. Sometimes the best place to start is with brutal honesty."

The natural tendency of human beings is to see themselves in the best light and blame others for the problems they face. Is it hard to admit that we do that?

Yes. But is it the truth? Yes. The worst part about that is how people try to "fix" these problems. People believe if they start over in a new area or get a new friend, spouse, house, job, car, etc., all of their problems will magically disappear. After obtaining what they want, however, their problems remain. Why?

The common denominator still remains: them.

It can be a difficult thing to be honest with ourselves. To sit back, have an honest conversation and say, "You're the problem, self." Dr. Jim Dittmar says, "When things go wrong; look in the mirror. When things go right; look out the window." To have success in your business or anything else in life, you must take personal responsibility. Don't wait for someone else to come along and fix things because you'll be waiting forever.

You have to be the leader you want to follow: That begins by being honest with yourself.

You didn't start a new business because things are exactly the way you want them to be. You started this business because you think things could be better. Good for you. By the way, you're right! Things can always be better.

If you are going to get to where you want to be you are going to have to change— and change often. Change isn't a bad thing, change is exciting! It begins with your mindset. Start by believing in your dreams and abilities.

Visualize yourself reaching your goals and objectives. Get excited about the opportunity to influence and change lives. Understand your dreams and aspirations can and will happen if you will change.

WHERE TO START

You must begin by asking these 4 questions and sub-questions:

WHO AM I?

- What are my greatest strengths and weaknesses?
- What do I like about myself?
- What don't I like about myself?

WHERE AM I?

- What location and period of time?
- What is my level of happiness on a scale of 1-10?
- Where am I along my path of life?
- If I asked myself ten years ago where I would be today, am I where I expected to be?

WHAT IS WRONG?

- What is wrong with who I am?
- What is wrong with where I am?

HOW CAN IT BE FIXED?

- How can I change?
- Where am I going?

A Chinese proverb says "Understanding is hard, but once one understands change is simple."

CHANGE YOURSELF

Change is a choice. You have to make a decision that you are going to be the best you can be regardless of what people are doing around you. Do what you've always done and get what you've always got. Do something different and you can expect something new and something worth fighting for.

If you are negative start being positive; if you are broke find a way to make more money. If you have been unsuccessful hang around successful people. If you want to learn more than educate yourself.

- Be a celebrator instead of a complainer.
- Be an encourager instead of a life drainer.
- Say positive things instead of negative things.
- Hope instead of despairing.
- Love instead of hate.
- Be open minded instead of closed minded.
- Be forgiving instead of bitter.
- Wake up earlier instead of later.
- Make progress instead of excuses.
- Be a winner instead of a loser.
- Be a champion instead of a winner.
- Be a life changer instead of a bump on a log.

Change is a *choice*. God has given you the ability to be the best you possible, but you have to be the one that walks through the open doors presented to you. Don't settle for less when you can have the best. Be the leader you would follow.

The choice is yours.

PICK A NEW DESTINATION

All leaders have two things in common: 1) they know where they're going and 2) they influence others to go with them. Jim Rohn says charting a new destination is simple, you do it by picking a new path and you start going that way. Pick your destination, believe with all of your heart that you will reach it, and tell others with the conviction of a giant that you will reach your destination.

You must believe you will reach your destination. Belief is the beginning of all great things. Columbus didn't inspire others to follow him into the unknown without belief. Alexander the Great did not lead an army to conquer the world without belief. Jesus did not change the world without belief. If you do not believe in where you are going, no one will follow.

John Maxwell says, "A leader's greatest opportunity is today." Let this be a challenge to you to make a choice today to change and change often. Lead others with love and encouragement. Show them a new course for their lives by going towards yours.

Be the leader you would follow.

THE TRUTH MUST WIN OUT

"I cannot tell a lie," summed up the value structure of one of the greatest U.S. presidents: Abraham Lincoln. His reputation for being honest deemed him the nickname "Honest Abe."

It can be tempting to stretch the truth when it comes to our business. Anyone who tells you otherwise hasn't done much in this industry. Scripture tells us "a good reputation is more desirable than great riches; to be esteemed is better than silver or gold." If you do not have a good reputation in this industry you have nothing. Take the example of Honest Abe and be honest even if you think if it will hurt your business.

Do not tell people you can get them a deal if you can't. Do not speak matter-of-factly unless you are 100 percent certain you can back up your word. If you can't get the best deal for your potential customer, let them know and give them the option to buy elsewhere. People are smart. You won't get away with being underhanded in your business. It's not guaranteed that being honest will lead to more sales. However, if you are dishonest, your business will fall apart.

One of the best phrases to master is "Sir or Ma'am, I don't know the answer to that, but I will find out and let you know." Too often we feel like we have to know everything. It is important for us to know as much as we can about our business. What makes a professional a professional is their ability to *find answers* and deliver those answers as promised. Don't be discouraged when you don't know something, it's just another opportunity to learn something new.

Truth is your most valuable asset; allow it to guide you in determining why you're doing this business.

DETERMINING YOUR WHY

Why you are doing this business is more important than how to do this business. Your "why" is more about what you want to become than what you would like to achieve. When difficulties arise or focus is lost, your "why" will keep on track. The following section will help you determine why you are doing this business.

Write down three to five reasons why you are doing this business. Some examples are as follows:

- Want to be debt free
- Want to have financial freedom so I can travel whenever I'd like
- Want to give to the poor
- Want to have money for my kids to go to college
- Want to start a community resource center
- Want to start a business without taking out a loan

Also include examples of what you don't want when determining your "why":

- I don't want to have a boss
- I don't want to have to wake up at 5:30 a.m. every morning to go to work
- I don't want to be scared to use my debit/credit card

- I don't want $200.00 to be a big deal to me
- I don't want to feel tight about money anymore
- I don't want to have a life that I think negatively about money

To determine your overall "why," look at the tangible items that you want or don't want such as "I don't want a boss," or "I want a new truck."

Now, close your eyes and imagine you have all of the things you want and you don't have the things you don't want. You are 100 percent debt-free and you have plenty of money in the bank to last you a very long time.

What will you do with your time and money? Who would you help? What changes would you make in the world?

The answer to these questions is your "why." For lasting success in this business it is vital to know why you are doing this.

You must make it habit to look at your "why" daily and refine the list as you check things off. Programming our minds towards what we want to happen and what will happen is important to our success.

GETTING DOWN TO BUSINESS

Now that you have determined why you are doing this business it is time to become an educated professional.

The high-level training on the following pages has the potential to transform you into a well-informed business person if it's properly applied. Don't skim the material and assume you know and understand all of the information. You must study it often.

The definition of the word "study" is "the application of the mind to the acquisition of knowledge, as by reading, investigation, or reflection. The cultivation of a particular branch of learning, science, or art: long hours of study." The reason we study is to become better professionals to lead to greater wealth, health, and spiritual growth. To do more, we have to become more.

Psychologists have done numerous studies on cognitive programming. One interesting study is in the area of Neuro-linguistic Programming (NLP). The theory is simple; the information you feed your mind determines the behaviors that will result. What we think is what we feel is what we do. In order to think properly we must program our minds with good information that will lead us to becoming who we want to be in business and in life. To be successful in business we must become ardent students of business. The more we learn the better we will become and the more we'll have to offer our customers and team members.

STARTING BLOCKS

We start our business with a tremendous amount of excitement which gives you the added push towards your first promotion. Often times, new representatives use up all of their excitement with nothing to fall back on.

We are going to give you steps to take to get you thinking, walking, and talking like a business owner even after excitement fades.

STEP 1: Business Cards

How many business owners do you know who write down their phone number and email address on a scratch piece of paper to give to prospective clients? None. Ordering business cards or making them yourself is important. When you have business cards it makes you look and feel professional instantly. It is your first mark as a business person.

Give your cards to everyone you know. Your business and you are one and the same. Everyone you know should know what you're doing. If you are at a bowling alley, church, American Legion, restaurant, grocery store, or anywhere with a bulletin board, your cards should be there. Get your name out everywhere.

Adding a picture to your business cards increases its effectiveness. Don't underestimate the power of facial recognition. The perception people have of you is their reality. If your business cards look professional and your face is on them, people will think of you in light of that.

STEP 2: Blogs and Vlogs

Over 180-million Americans log onto the Internet daily. Of those 180-million people, how many do you know? Probably about half-a-percent at best. That leaves 99-and-a-half percent or 179.95-million people you haven't met.

How do we get to know them? Go where they go: the Internet.

Blogs and "vlogs" (or video blogs) are the simplest way to build credibility and network online. Pick a topic that you like— preferably a topic about your business—and begin posting at minimum three times per week. In order to pick the topic for your blog or vlog ask this question: What would I like to become the expert in? Is it a product or service? Is it business building techniques? Is it relationship building? Pick the topic that best suits you and start blogging regularly.

BLOGGING BASICS

It is important that you keep proper syntax when writing your blog. Here are a few good rules to follow:

- The blog should be 250-500 words. Anything shorter does not typically give enough information and anything longer might lose the reader's attention.
- The blog should never include curse words or offensive language
- The blog should remain objective and stray from heavy opinion on controversial topics
- The blog should site resources appropriately (for information on citing sources, visit www.citationmachine.net)

EXAMPLE OF A BLOG

Blog used by permission. Mainstream Life Solutions, LLC

Have you ever heard this saying: First you form your **habits** and then your habits form you? Nothing could be truer; so many of us are a product of our habits. Think about it. What if suddenly your water was shut off due to a natural catastrophe and you couldn't take a shower or brush your teeth; you would be completely out of sorts. Some of us would lose our minds because hygiene is very important to us. Brushing our teeth, washing our face, taking showers, drinking water, eating, etc. are all habits to us. We usually don't have to wake up pondering what approach we'll take in washing our hair. We are innate about it. We don't give it a second thought. Why? It's a habit we've formed over many years.

What are some other habits we have? Driving a car, making coffee in the morning, going to school, washing the dishes, so on and so forth; we could go on for days talking about some of the necessary habits we have in order to function efficiently. Our habits truly do form who we become. We must develop positive character habits if we are going to be successful.

A few years ago I developed a simple habit of picking up trash whenever I saw it. Unfortunately, I don't always **focus** on seeing trash, but when I do I've been consistent in picking it up. In fact, just the other day I was driving to the office and a big bag of trash was lying in the middle of the road.

This wasn't a back road; it was a state route so the bag was dangerous to the drivers. Everyone was slowing down and driving around it.

Without much hesitation I turned around, went back and put the stinky, slimy bag in my trunk, drove to the office and threw it in the bin.

Prior to developing my habit of picking up trash, I would have driven by without a sideways glance or thought. However, because I developed this habit with small pieces of trash here and there, the big stuff didn't bother me. One of my goals is to leave the world in better shape than when I was brought into it. Picking up trash fits into that goal. Therefore, it's a no brainer.

What are some positive **habits** you have? What are some that you would like to develop? I'd like to urge you to developing positive habits one step at a time. It's easy to form bad habits; it takes conscious effort and work to develop good ones. Join me in cleaning up our world.

Did you notice the paragraph spacing and the sentence structure? Did you notice some words are highlighted and underlined? That is called linking which we will talk about later in this section.

Blogs are not meant to be philosophical discourses or research reports; they are short, informative pieces meant for continuing readership. Your goal is to get subscribers to follow your blog consistently.

Whichever topic you choose, make sure you get books, articles, and videos on the topic; interview experts and get detailed information. Become the expert.

SOCIAL MEDIA

Social media is one of the best tools for building credibility. The information people post on their social media sites tells a lot about their character and values. If you have not used social media or have used it sparingly, that's okay.

We are going to map out a social media game plan that will help build and maintain credibility for you and your business.

WHERE TO START

You must first decide what you want to use social media for. Are you going to use your site for promoting a product or service? Do you want to promote yourself and the business? Would you like to use social media to promote your expertise in a certain field? The answer to that question will greatly affect your strategy. The most important thing to remember about social media is—it is all about relationships. Pastor Mike Ross says, "Relationships are the bridges over which values are transferred." Do not use social media as an advertising medium; you will be ignored and lose friends as quick as you get them. These are a few good ways to build your credibility through social media.

1. *Reach out*
    Do not wait for people to "friend" you. Use the smart tools in your social media outlet and find friends that are in the same industry as

you. Type in "Networking", "Network Marketing", "Direct Selling", "Marketing", "Advertising", etc. When the search results come up, "friend request" people you would like to know.

2. *Follow the "15-minutes-a-day" rule*

Social media does not have to be time consuming. A great rule is to take 15 minutes each day to seek out new friends. Another great rule is to have a set number of friends you would like to add every day. For instance, let's say five is your set number. After you have "friended" five people, get on their page and learn a little bit about them. Then, write them a short private message that only they will see. Say something like, "Hey friend, I see you are in network marketing, that's great! I love the industry and wanted to reach out and meet more like-minded people. How are things going for you in your business?" Make sure you make it brief, leaving the conversation open and easy for them to respond.

3. *Link to your blog*

An excellent way to get readership on your blog and to build credibility through social media is by linking your blog to your social media site. Some blogging platforms, like Wordpress, automatically spits out a link on your social media sites once a new post is added to your blog (given that you've properly linked your social media sites to your blog). Some blogging platforms require you to manually "copy and paste" the link on your social media pages each time you post a blog. When people see you are a serious blogger, your following will grow.

4. *Be positive*

Don't "vent" on your social media site. Don't post anything you wouldn't want your boss, pastor, or mother to see. Nothing will destroy your credibility faster than venting frustrations on the front of your social media sites. Instead, make it a habit of complimenting others posts and saying encouraging things to others as often as possible.

5. *Pictures and videos*

   Don't put pictures or videos on your social media site that you wouldn't show your boss, pastor, or mother. Pictures with your middle-finger pointing to the sky, you with a 32-oz. beer and glazed eyes, and raunchy bump-and-grind photos or videos need to be prohibited from your site. Instead, put a handful of pictures on the site representing your professionalism.

6. *Do not neglect*

   Social media is a "what-have-you-done-for-me-lately" medium. Yesterday's posts are quickly forgotten and people are on to the next exciting thing. Be sure to do something with social media every day.

As you grow in your social networking skills, you will find it is fairly easy to keep up with. Today's technology is built around social media. One word of warning to save you from getting wrapped into the social media vortex: Have set times every day that you will visit your social media pages. Do not allow it to dominate your life.

HAVING A WEB SITE

If you were shopping for a suit in the city and you came to a four way intersection and saw a storefront tailor and next to the store was a street tailor with nothing more than a table, a rack of suits, and a measuring tape, which tailor would you choose?

The majority would choose the storefront. Why? The storefront gives us security that the business owner had a plan; having a building to walk into gives us a sense the business owner is a professional and cares enough about customers to give them cover for their heads.

A Web site is like having a store front on the web. It's amazing how many businesses do not have Web sites or the sites they do have are unattended or shoddy. It's important to have and maintain a Web site as a business owner. A Web site, like social media and blogs, adds to your credibility and gives you a place for revenue streams. Here is a simple step-by-step process for developing your own website.

STEP 1: Secure a URL (Uniform Resource Locator)
This is your "www-dot-something." As simple as a URL is; it can make or break your Web site. One concrete piece of advice is to have more than one URL. The price of a URL is very low (usually between ten and 20 dollars), therefore purchasing many isn't out of the question.

Let's say you are a representative of a cosmetics company. Think of a URL your customers will not forget like. A few examples are www.splashcosmetics.com, www.myfacefeelsgreat.com, www.wavyhair.net, or a funny URL, www.myhairaintnappy.com. A great rule of thumb is to secure a URL that is spelled like it sounds. Avoid big and uncommon words. To secure your URL go to www.register.com, www.1and1.com, www.godaddy.com or any URL-securing sites.

After securing your URL, try also to secure the ".net," ".org," ".cc," ".us" of the same name. Also, secure as many misspelled URL's of your name as you can. You will be amazed the kind of traffic you can receive on your site from misspelled words. When you finish purchasing your URL's you will be ready to move to the next step.

STEP 2: Create content

Nothing drives web developers or marketing professionals crazier than customers that don't have content ready for their site. You may be thinking, "What content should I put on my site?"
Use the K.I.S.S. principle: keep it short and simple. You can expect the average person to leave your site in seconds unless something grabs them. Ask yourself, "What intrigued me about my business after I first saw the plan?" It may have been the freedom or the money or the relationships attainable through the business opportunity. Whatever it was, make that your starting point. The following are some good tips for great content:

1. *Spacing*
    Space your sentences and paragraphs accordingly. Think about the websites you visit regularly. Most of them are easy on your eyes, aren't they? Format your site so that it's "easy on the eyes."

2. *Simplicity*
    The content of your homepage should be simple; give the visitor just enough content to interest them. The real content should be on your clickable links. Also, do not use superfluous words. Wait, what's superfluous? Exactly the point. Use words that everyone will follow.

3. *Conversational tones*

    When you write content for your Web site, write as if you are talking to a close friend. The less rigid, the better.

    STEP 3: Look and feel

    The look and feel of your site is just as important as the content. This is why we suggest you go to a professional like crunchypixel.com or coldxpressions.com for your Web site needs. A professional can give you examples to choose from and help you decide what's best for you. If you choose not to go to a professional, here are some suggestions for you:

1. *If you don't know, don't go*

    Often times we settle for things we're not completely sold on. When it comes to your Web site only publish it if you are 100 percent about the look and feel. Don't settle for second best, because your Web site will be your first impression on many people.

2. *Pick from your favorites*

    What Web sites do you visit? Do you like the look and feel? *You don't have to reinvent the wheel.* Take a couple websites you like and formulate the look and feel of your Web site based on those. Your Web site will be innovative because it is yours.

3. *Ask someone*

    Call your friends and family members and ask them to give you an honest opinion of your site before you launch. Humans have flaws and we can under or overestimate. The opinions of those closest to you will help tremendously. Try not to get offended if they don't like it, graciously accept constructive criticism.

4. *Be careful*

    People build their own Web sites for two reasons: 1) they want to save money or 2) they believe they can build it "their way." A word of advice – Do your homework! Make sure you know how much time and money you will spend using a Web site building tool. Often times you will save money by hiring a professional.

    STEP 4: The Launch

    This is the fun part of having a Web site. Once you have everything in place call your friends, family, co-workers and team members. Post links on all your social media pages. Make flyers, secure billboards, put it on your business cards and link it to your blog. Do whatever it takes (within legal limits) to drive traffic to your Web site. Have fun with this part, but make sure you do not neglect. Update the content of your site regularly.

    Building your business starts with a solid foundation. You must be solid personally or the foundation of your business will fall apart. Before you are ready to venture into the face-to-face aspect of network marketing, be sure to utilize the online tools of this chapter to establish your credibility

CHAPTER 4
BUILDING A NETWORK

Networking is an essential part of building wealth.

Armstrong Williams

In the film *Family Man,* Nicholas Cage makes a powerful statement, "I know business; it is nothing more than people waking up every day trying to pay for their kids' college education." Business is people and people are business. To be successful in business we must learn the art of building and maintaining relationships. People are complex and no two are the same. However, people do share similarities categorized as personality types.

In his book Positive Personality Profiles, Dr. Robert Rohm breaks down peoples personalities into four letters: D,I, S and C. The "D" personalities are dominant, driving, demanding, determined, decisive, and doers. The "I" personalities are inspirational, influencing, inducing, impressive, interactive, interesting, and interested. The "S" personalities are supportive, submissive, stable, steady, sentimental, shy, status-quo, and specialists. The "C" personalities are cautious, competent, calculating, concerned, careful, and contemplative.

Just by looking at these words we could name a person we know who fits each category. Most people are a combination of two or three personality types. It is important to understand what category people fit into so we can relate to each person we meet. Knowing products and services is 20 percent of your business, knowing people is 80 percent. Spend more time studying people rather than products and services.

Regardless of personality type, all people have one thing in common: the innate desire to feel important. Attempts at manipulation because of people's desire will backfire. People are savvier than they've ever been and can easily sense when a person is trying to use them to make a quick buck. The way to build lasting success is by developing a genuine desire to build lasting relationships.

IT BEGINS IN YOU

Do you have the best view of yourself? Why or why not? Our view of ourselves determines our view of the world. Psychological scientist Ivan Pavlov was the father of classical conditioning. He conducted experiments to discover why humans react the way they do in various circumstances. Conditioning is the process of learning associations. In classical conditioning, we learn to associate two stimuli and thus anticipate outcomes or reactions.

For instance, if you look into the sky and see dark clouds forming, your mind immediately connects stimuli preparing you to do what you're conditioned to do when it rains. You may find shelter, get an umbrella, or get your dancing shoes on (if you like to dance in the rain). The clouds might also alter your mood. If you don't like rain, the rain clouds may cause you to feel depressed. Your mind is conditioned to think certain ways based on your experiences and thought patterns.

The concept of classical conditioning is vital for us to understand as business owners. How we react to crisis, deal with our teams, conduct interviews and sell products is all a direct result of our conditioned thought patterns. This poem shared by Mark Matteson in his book *Freedom from Fear Forever* puts it simply:

> Watch your thoughts, they become your words
> Watch your words, they become your actions;
> Watch your actions, they become your habits;
> Watch your habits, they become your character;
> Watch your character, for it becomes your destiny.
> It all starts with your thoughts.

After reading this, ask yourself again, "What is my view of myself?" Most people become mentally challenged towards the idea of success because of negative experiences.

Let's see if we can address a few bad experiences and address the underlying assumptions our minds make because of them.

EXAMPLE 1

Experience: Rejection – A person we love and admire criticized you harshly for trying something new that is out of the ordinary. Some examples may be skydiving, going on a road trip, getting a tattoo or voting for a new political party.

Reaction: You are hurt or discouraged. You feel like you've offended and are now out of good graces with a person you love and admire. Your emotions become unstable and you want a resolution.

Possible learned behaviors: Negative self-talk (conscious or unconscious) such as "Don't try anything out of the ordinary", "I'm stupid for doing that", "You can't take risks or you'll lose all of your friends" or "My worth is based on the opinions of others."

The truth: The person who criticized you had an opinion and probably reacted negatively based on their own negative experience. Their behavior was learned and is a poor standard to base your life on. Your value and self-worth is not predicated on what others think about you. You aren't stupid or wrong for trying something new.

EXAMPLE 2

Experience: Car accident – You were driving in the snow and you slid off the road and crashed into a median. You were not severely injured but had a few cuts and bruises.

Reaction: You are in pain and shock. Your body is in pain and you've lost your car. You have to make adjustments to your lifestyle for a short period until you get a new car.

Possible learned behavior: Fear of driving. You become shaky every time you drive around a bend for fear that you will slide off the road. You avoid going places and cancel appointments because you want to reduce the risk of another accident.

The truth: Accidents are out of the ordinary. The road conditions the day you wrecked were out of the ordinary. You are a good driver and should be as careful as possible, but have nothing to fear when it comes to getting back on the road.

EXAMPLE 3

Experience: Public Speaking – You were doing a speech in front of a class and you stuttered, stammered, and forgot what you planned to say.

Reaction: Humiliation. Your face is red and hot. You feel about the size of an amoeba and have the serious urge to vomit.

Possible learned behavior: Avoidance .You never, ever, ever, ever want to experience that kind of humiliation again. You go out of your way to make sure you never have to speak publicly again. You become uncomfortable outside of your established friend and family circles.

The truth: People don't care – Ask yourself this question: When you've seen a person screw up a speech (unless it was of epic proportions), how long did you really think about it afterwards? Not for very long. The truth is people think about themselves about 95 percent of the time and most of the time and only care what you say if it pertains to their lives. There is absolutely nothing to fear when speaking publicly because people don't care as much as you think.

The examples given here are not out of the ordinary. They were taken from real-life scenarios. As business owners we must condition our minds to react in positive ways. We are responsible for our conditioning. This is where change is exciting. Take inventory of your thought processes and challenge negative thoughts and behaviors that are based on unordinary experiences or other people's opinions. Base your life on truth. Lies are pervasive and easy to find, but truth must be sought out. Living by truth is the gateway to effective relationship building.

Building effective relationships begins by thinking the best of everyone. You can't do that to your full potential unless you think the best of yourself. Don't you find it peculiar that we are quick to encourage others when they are having a hard day, but when it comes to ourselves we'd rather kick when we're down? Give yourself a break. Many times we are harder on ourselves than others. In some circumstances, that's good but we must keep a positive perspective. You are a masterpiece. Condition your mind to believe it.

HOW TO BECOME A GREAT NETWORKER

You must become a master at building real, down-to-earth relationships to become a great networker. No one likes to go to networking events to get solicited to. Again, it's easy to spot a smarmy sales person who cares only about your pocket book. Those people are a dime a dozen. We want you to become excellent at building relationships. To become excellent you must C-R-E-A-T-E an internal awareness of others.

C – Care for them

You cannot be insincere and have lasting impact on people. You must have a genuine love and compassion for people if you are going to be a great networker. Get past the surface and find out about people's lives. People enjoy talking about themselves. Ask as many questions as you can when you first meet a person. A good rule of thumb is to save the personal questions until after you have discussed business, interests, education, goals and dreams. Certain people don't like discussing family with business contacts. Just be aware of this and play it by ear.

R – Relate to people

Find things you have in common and use them to relate to people. The person you're speaking to may like a particular type of music that you like. Try to stay on that topic for a while. When you discuss similar interests you develop the common ground needed for enriching and refreshing conversation. Find as many similar interests as possible.

However, be careful not to skim over the things you are not interested in. The best way to learn about a new topic is by asking someone who knows about it. You can earn a high-level education just through asking questions and listening.

E – Energize people

Nothing energizes people more than great compliments. Be intentional about finding things to compliment people about. Would you be surprised to know that some people go months without getting good, sincere compliments? It is easy to find the good in everyone if you are intentional about it. Another way to energize people is by smiling, laughing, and having a positive spirit. This is called charisma. Charisma is a choice. We choose whether or not we're going to have a good day or bad day and how we use our face. We have the choice to be inviting or uninviting. Choose to be inviting and it will bless others. It pays huge dividends to train yourself to be positive.

A – Affirm people

Dale Carnegie used to teach his classes to be "hearty in their approbation and lavish in their praise." When you are getting to know people and discovering their goals, dreams, and desires it is important to affirm the things they want out of life.

Go the extra mile to tell people why you believe their dreams are great. It takes no effort to talk about ourselves, but it takes sincere effort to dig deeper into the lives of others. Consequently, few things are more rewarding. People need affirmation. Use your gifts, talents, and abilities to give it freely.

T – Talk about people

Gossip is a disease in our culture. Talking negatively about someone behind their back is one of the most despicable things we can do. On the other hand, talking positively about people behind their back and in front of them is one of the most uplifting and emotionally beneficial things you can do. When you speak positively about other people you start thinking positively about other people. How many times have you caught someone talking good about you? Doesn't it feel great? Be the one that gets caught speaking well about others.

E – Establish people

When you've taken the time to get to know someone at an event or function it is important that you establish the person as a contact or a friend. Leave the conversation a bit open and set up a time for coffee or lunch or an activity of similar interest (golf, crochet, bingo, etc.). Do not leave the conversation until you have established that you will be talking again. This is called follow-up and is an important part of being a successful networker.

NETWORKING AND REFERRALS

Now that we have discussed the process for building relationships it is important that we develop a strategy for networking.

We recommend going to as many networking events, meetings or groups as possible. Some well known networking opportunities around the country are BNI (Business Networking International), Rotary, Chamber, Lions Club, The Elks, Country Clubs, YMCA, and many more. Take a stack of business cards to each meeting and practice the C.R.E.A.T.E system.

Have a game plan when you go to a new event such as meeting twenty new people and establishing two solid contacts. Whatever you do: plan. Most of us are familiar with the quote, "Those who fail to plan, plan to fail."

That is an absolute truth in business. Dr. Maxwell says, "Preparation is the key to sustaining momentum." Planning doesn't take long, but it does take effort, focus and application.

TRADESHOWS

Attend tradeshows as often as possible. Tradeshows give you the opportunity to get in front of thousands of people in a short period of time. It can be expensive to buy a booth or table at a tradeshow, but the return on investment is worth the business cost. You will get in front of many people you normally couldn't in a short period of time. If the tradeshow is too expensive for you, we suggest getting one (or many) of your partners to invest in the trade show with you. There will be plenty of people for all of you to talk to.

When attending tradeshows it is important to set up a way to gather information. You will need to develop lead-generation information cards.

This could be anything from a piece of paper that asks for name and email address to professionally produced cards that ask name, address, phone number, email, and a few survey questions. Our suggestion; spare no expense and get the most information you can. Remember, these events may be all about impression, you want the best impression made with as many people you can.

Location is vital. Where you are set up within the arena will determine on the success you will have. If the show is in a larger arena, you need to plan carefully. Make sure you get a copy of the floor plan of the arena prior to purchasing a booth.

Most shows will allow you to pick precisely where you would like to be set up. You want to be seen by at least 80 percent of the people that enter the arena. Where you are located will be a largely impact your success.

Your display is the second most important factor of success when it comes to trade shows. Do not settle for something cheap and forgettable. Do something extraordinary! Go for entertainment and mystery. If the tradeshow allows, set up a booth that can be closed in a certain area and allow only those who fill out information cards to enter. You will be surprised how popular a booth can become among the audience if you provide a bit of entertainment and mystery. Also, if you can, take an extra computer monitor or television and create a power point to explain briefly what your company is about. You do not want to spend the day explaining your business; that should be saved for other encounters.

It's all about the hellos and goodbyes. You may only get 5 seconds with a person at these events. You must be smiling and excited every time you see a new face. Greet people with enthusiastic hellos and goodbyes. Make a great first impression.

If you are not sure where to find tradeshow opportunities, ask local business people or search online.

SEMINARS

Networking events and trade shows are for promoting your business. Seminars are for educating the public. Earlier, we discussed the importance of branding yourself online.

Seminars are for branding yourself face-to-face. Here is a step-by-step process for having an effective seminar.

STEP 1: Pick a topic

Your topic is the most important feature of your seminar. Your topic should be broad enough to interest many people but focused enough to intrigue industry-specific professionals. Make sure it is a topic you are already comfortable with. You want to teach people from your own personal experience and not the experience of others. This is why new representatives should wait until they have had some success before holding a seminar.

STEP 2: Pick the players

Who, besides yourself, would you like to speak at your seminar?

People in sales professions love to get in front of an audience because it gives them credibility and a chance to network. A word of caution: Be careful in choosing speakers. Do your "due diligence" by asking them to provide references for you to call to ensure their credibility. If you have someone speaking at your event that has a bad reputation, people will not attend regardless of how much they like you. Do not assume someone has credibility; just because you know them personally or they attend your church doesn't mean they have a good business reputation.

STEP 3: Pick the location and date

When picking location think of where the majority of your audience will be coming from. Try the best you can to ensure no one will have to drive over 20 minutes to your event.

The date is also very important. Typically the best day of the week is Thursday evening. Thursdays work well because people are still in "business mode" but in the back of their mind they know the weekend is one work day away.

STEP 4: Pick your promoters

Use your team to promote your event. Have your team invite as many people as possible. Make flyers with the topic, the speakers, the location and date. Take the flyers everywhere you can. You will also want to write a press release to submit to local papers. Press releases are free advertising for your event they establish credibility for what you are doing. Start promoting at least a month in advance for your event.

WEBINARS

Webinars are short, online seminars and are a powerful business building tool. A majority of companies use webinars for in-house training and information but webinars can be effectively used in many different ways. Monetizing webinars has become increasingly popular in many industries, particularly network marketing. Webinars can become a new stream of income, help with branding and build credibility. Webinars are especially useful when building customer bases and teams in different areas of the country and world. Webinars should be promoted and used in the same format as seminars.

THE IMPORTANCE OF FOLLOW UP

Do not underestimate the power of follow up. Think about it for a second. How often have you met someone, had a great conversation and nothing ever materialized out of it? This happens all the time because most people are not proactive in following up. After you realize how simple follow-up is, you should never miss another opportunity. Relationships aren't built upon one gigantic cord, but by thousands of tiny cords stranded together. Think of cards, phone calls, and meetings as tiny cords in your relationships. It doesn't take a lot of time, but it does take effort.

After you meet someone at an event take some time the next day or the day after to follow up either through a hand written note or a phone call. Dr. Don Vollmer suggests if a person is a top level prospect to send them priority mail with some information and a hand written note. Dr. Vollmer says, "This method of delivery is always opened."
Just the same, cards, notes, and phone calls are well received. When following up, be sure to remember important things about your conversation that will connect your prospect back to you.

Suggest in your note or call a time when you can get together for another conversation. Tell them how much you enjoy talking to them and ensure them you feel you could learn something from them. A wise sage once said, "You can learn something from a toddler if they have something to say that you don't know." Be open to learning from as many people as possible and you will gain more friends and prospects.

Don't allow more than three days to pass before you follow up. People are busy and they forget faces and names quickly. After a tradeshow where you've make hundreds of contacts, you may want to hire someone to help you write the same hand-written note over and over again. Sign the bottom of each note yourself and send it to your prospects. The note still has the same power, but will eliminate the time it takes to personally write and address each one.

Direct mail is still well received when it is made personal. No one likes to get "sale mail" or endless flyers, but most everyone appreciates thoughtful, hand-written letters. Avoid using email or sending information through email until after you have established a second connection. Email is a great tool and should be utilized effectively. Notify your prospect that you will be sending them an email before you do it. If you do not, your email may get deleted or blocked.

Never forget that people are business and business is people. If you can master the art of human relations you will go far in your business. Once you do, you will be ready to build teams that achieve lasting success.

CHAPTER 5

TEAM BUILDING

Finding good players is easy. Getting them to play as a team is

another story.

Casey Stengel

Have you ever wondered why some teams are great, some are mediocre and others are terrible? Is it talent? No, talent may have a bit to do with it, but some of the most talented teams are just average by the numbers. Is it coaching? Well, coaching has a bit to do with it but that's not it either. So what is it that makes a team?

Let's see what the dictionary definition is:

1. A number of persons forming one of the sides in a game or contest: *a football team.*

2. A number of persons associated in some joint action: *a team of advisers.*

Here's what some experts have to say about the make-up of a team: "There is no I in Team." – John Wooden

"Teamwork divides the task and doubles the success." – Joe Paterno

"Teamwork is the ability to work together toward a common vision. The ability to direct individual accomplishments toward organizational objectives. It is the fuel that allows common people to attain uncommon results." - Vince Lombardi

For your team to grow you must take leadership. Leadership is influencing others through the highest standards of excellence in faith, character, and initiative towards common goals and shared ideas.

Have you noticed the word "common" being used a lot? Network marketing requires common goals and team accomplishment for success. As the leader it will be your job to find the commonalities within your network marketing community. If your team doesn't have an established culture you will have to build it. The book *Organizational Culture and Leadership* by Dr. Edgar Schein explains how to establish a culture. According to Schein a culture is established in three ways.

1. *Through artifacts.*

   Artifacts are things you can see, touch, and hold. The place where your team meets on a regular basis, the training books you use, the products or services that make up your business are all artifacts of your culture. Be sure to create artifacts that have your team values written on them to reinforce organizational culture.

2. *Through espoused beliefs and values.*

   To achieve your vision you must establish beliefs and values that will benefit everyone while giving careful thought to the production of the entire team.

3. *Through underlying assumptions.*

   Underlying assumptions are the unspoken rules of the team. Many times underlying assumptions are established through artifacts and espoused beliefs. For instance, if an espoused value is to commit to all Tuesday evening training meetings, the underlying assumption of the team is you don't plan anything on Tuesday evenings.

After you understand the three levels of culture it becomes easy to know how your team functions. If changes need to be made you'll know which of the three levels to address. Most changes occur in espoused beliefs and values.

In the beginning stages of growing our direct selling business, we had no defined standard of production and great value was placed upon individual accomplishments. We announced and recognized the few people who had the highest numbers month after month and people who were at the bottom of the totem pole became discouraged and stopped trying.

We realized we needed to change our system and establish a culture that had the best interests of everyone in mind. We focused on educating each individual and establishing attainable monthly goals. Because we changed the values of our team, our artifacts such as the books and material we based our training on changed, too.

The unspoken rules or underlying assumptions became "no one is left behind." Updating and understanding values is one of the most important aspects of team building.

THE IMPORTANCE OF VISION

No task is more important to a leader than casting a vision for their team. We're not talking about dreams for your team; visions and dreams are two different things. To have a successful network marketing organization you must become a visionary who develops visionaries. In his book *Visioneering,* Andy Stanley says "Dreamers dream about things being different. Visionaries envision themselves making a difference. Dreamers think about how nice it would be for something to be done. Visionaries look for an opportunity to do something."

A leader does not dream about what *could* be; they are already walking towards what *will* be.

You may have a big vision for yourself. Earlier in the book we wrote down our "whys" or our personal reasons for wanting success. To establish a vision for your team find the common things your team wants and develop a vision based upon those things.

We have been extremely blessed to have great-hearted individuals on our team. The common "whys" of our team are things like, "We want to be free to spend more time with our families" "We want to have an abundance to help our community build resource centers, bridges, homeless shelters." "We want to help destroy generational poverty." This represents just a few. And yes, individuals on our team want to buy houses, cars, vacations, rental houses, etc. However, those things are secondary. We function as if those things will come as we set out to make a difference in world.

Take inventory of your team and see where their hearts are at. Effective visions are based upon making a lasting difference. What are problems in your community that money could change? What would happen if your team decided to create a fund where everyone on the team could donate 10 percent of all their business profits in order to give back to the community? Do you believe that would help achieve individual as well as team goals? Part of vision is finding what needs fixed and establishing a plan to fix it. It's not rocket science. Most of the time when a team gets together to fulfill a team vision, individual visions are also realized.

Cast a vision by gathering your team and ask what you could do together to make a difference. Even if you are the one casting the vision, including your team allows it to become their vision as well. Plus you never know who will mention something that will make achieving your vision easier. Listen to your team and be open to change. Remember, casting the vision doesn't make the vision yours—it makes you the leader. The vision is and should always be the organizational goal.

Find out what your team wants to become, and then establish goals to help you get there.

THE IMPORTANCE OF GOALS

Too many direct selling companies place emphasis on individual production. We've all heard the stories about the person who started their network marketing company and made 75-billion dollars in two months, retired and now owns six islands off the coast of Florida. Quite frankly, those stories get old. We're very happy for the people who have that kind of success and it's inspiring to know we all have the same opportunity. The facts are still the facts; in most situations it takes a tremendous amount of time and effort to build your business. Therefore, setting individual and team goals are very important to realizing your vision.

Goals must be attainable and agreed upon. For instance, let's assume you have 100 people on your team. You could set an individual goal of one new product or service per month and one new partner per month. That means the team goal would be 100 new products or services and 100 new partners. Once the goals are agreed upon then it's time to promote and motivate people towards the team goals. When people know they are working towards common goals the production is higher. According to Kouzes and Posner in their book *Encouraging the Heart*, hundreds of research studies clearly demonstrate that people will act consistently with our expectations. As the leader you must expect your team to accomplish the goals you agree upon and in the meantime people will accomplish their individual goals.

It is truly a win-win situation when leaders establish a vision and develop goals based upon that vision. Be sure to make the vision something grandiose and the goals attainable. The smaller the goals the greater the achievement, the greater the achievement, the greater the growth, the greater the growth, the closer you will get to your vision.

HOW TO KEEP YOUR TEAM FOCUSED

After you have established a vision and goals for you team you must establish a system for keeping everyone on the same page. We suggest developing the following team gatherings and support systems to keep constant reminders of individual responsibility.

Team is the most important aspect of your business. Your team must commit to being plugged in and invest time into growing their business. People that succeed in this industry take action. The training calls, training sessions, business presentations, and individual meetings are vital to seeing growth in your business.

BUSINESS PRESENTATIONS

Business Presentations are given to show prospective representatives the company overview and introduce them to the team. It's a good idea to establish weekly or monthly team presentations to give representatives the ability to show prospects the business opportunity in a supportive group setting. To be successful, team members must show up consistently, whether they have guests or not.

TRAINING MEETINGS

Training meetings should be held consistently to give team members new tools, materials and strategies to help their business grow. These meetings should cover all the basics of team building, customer gathering, practical business presentations and anything else necessary to help new and existing representatives acquire knowledge and grow in business savvy. These meetings also give each team member the opportunity to ask questions and glean from other members.

TRAINING CALLS

Training calls are for additional training and updates about your business. Each call should feature a successful business person who shares their secrets on team building.

3RD PARTY CALLS

When introducing your business to prospects, it's important to call or have someone with you who has experience. This will give you credibility and allow the prospect to speak with someone else who is enthusiastic about your business. This also allows your team leaders to mentor you on how to present the business and help you learn from possible mistakes.

PRESENTING YOUR BUSINESS STEP-BY-STEP

There are four basic steps to introducing your direct selling business to potential representatives. The first step is to set up an appointment to meet your prospect and present your business.

The second step is the introduction and it occurs at the appointment before you begin the business presentation.

The third step is the close of the presentation where you ask the prospect to become a representative or customer. The fourth step in presenting your business is overcoming objections, which will be addressed in the following chapter.

SECURING APPOINTMENTS

Appointments are opportunities for you to introduce your direct selling business to potential independent representatives or customers. To be successful in direct selling you need to know the basics of becoming a successful appointment-setter.

Be honest and straightforward when setting appointments. Many network marketing companies promote the "smoke and mirrors" approach to securing appointments.

A lot of direct selling "experts" suggest that you set appointments by being vague and nondescript. This tactic is birthed from the stigma of network marketing and is somewhat understandable. But instead of overcoming the stigma through education and professionalism, it adds to it by leaving your prospects feeling fooled and defensive. While in the short-term the "smoke and mirrors" approach to setting appointments may work, in the long-term it will damage your credibility and eliminate business-savvy prospects.

While securing appointments, convey your passion for your business. Remember that the business you are presenting has the potential to make the prospect a millionaire. Speak to them with that kind of enthusiasm.

Be up front about your intention of showing them a network marketing business opportunity. Your straightforwardness about your involvement in network marketing will show them that you're confident about the opportunity you're presenting and likely disarm them after the appointment is secured.

Don't try to explain your business over the phone; a face-to-face appointment is necessary to do justice to the opportunity you're presenting. Explaining a complex business over the phone will overwhelm your prospect and leave them confused. Could Bill Gates explain Microsoft over the phone or Sam Walton the concept behind Wal-Mart? Would Stephen Spielberg try to explain a movie plot over the phone? In the same way, you should save the explanations of your business for face-to-face encounters.

Practice and preparation will lead to greater success. Here are some statements to practice as you prepare to make phone calls and set appointments:

- "Hey Bill, it's Frida, I've gotten involved in a network marketing company that I'm really excited about. I really think you'd be impressed with the business plan and I'm calling to set up a meeting with you. Are you available for lunch tomorrow?"

- "Hi Sally, it's Fred. Are you available to meet tomorrow? I started a network marketing business that I'm excited to tell you about. I need about a half hour of your time to show you the business plan. I think you'll be really impressed."

- "Hey Raynaldo, it's Stacey. Would it be alright if I stopped by your office? I have an impressive network marketing business for you to take a look at."

Chances are you'll face obstacles and objections at the appointment setting stage. Some people will be apprehensive about meeting with you because of the stigma of the direct selling industry or negative past experiences. If this occurs, don't take it as a personal rejection. Instead, press on to set up the appointment and tell your prospect in a professional way how serious you are about building your business. You can practice the following statements to prepare for any resistance you might meet while setting appointments:

- "I'm sorry if you've had some bad experiences with network marketing in the past but I assure you I'm not calling to coerce or recruit you. I'm building this business in a big time way and, based on our relationship, I'd like you to take a look at the opportunity."
- "Are you apprehensive because this is network marketing? I understand that there are some negative perceptions about the industry but I'm involved in a solid company and part of a solid team. I'd really appreciate if you'd take an honest look at the opportunity."

After you've secured the appointment, the next step in presenting your business is the introduction of the presentation.

BEFORE THE PRESENTATION

Your goal before you present is to build rapport and disarm your

Prospect so that they are comfortable during the presentation. Business presentations can be stressful for you and for your prospect.

Brian Tracy, motivational speaker and author, says your job is to alleviate as much pressure as possible. Make the meeting fun, light and something that the prospect could see themselves doing. The more relaxed you are the more relaxed they will be. Here is an example of a good introduction:

"Tim and Mary thank you so much for letting me come and show you this business. I'm extremely excited about it and I think you will be too. Before we get going I have three questions for you.

One, if you stop working your job today or next week or next month would you ever get another paycheck? Two, if you were financially free, what would you do with your time? Three, I'm going to show you this presentation and I want you to know up front that it's ok if you tell me no. I'd just like you to keep an open mind. I hope that you do say yes because I think this is the greatest opportunity in the world. However, whatever you decide is okay with me. Is that fair?"

At this point, you will begin the business presentation.

THE PRESENTATION
What company you represent will determine the way you present your business. Many network marketing companies have presentations on video that are available for representatives to use.

In other cases, you may have to do the presentation yourself with a flip chart or slideshow. Make the presentation as simple as possible. If there are video presentations available through your particular company, use them. If you have to give the presentation yourself, make it pointed and brief but don't leave out any of the important details. Present the products and services the company offers, the company's pay plan and the cost to join. Also discuss any quotas or recurring costs.

It's important that your presentation makes it obvious that you are both excited and serious about your business. Present the business in such a way that it's a "no brainer" for your prospect. Highlight the awesome opportunities available through your company and assure them that no matter what they choose, you will continue to build your business and reach your goals. That type of confidence will ignite their confidence in you.

CLOSING THE PRESENTATION

At this point you will ask your prospect to make a decision about whether or not they will join your business and become a representative or customer. You will want to start the close by getting your prospect to answer "yes" to a few questions before you asking them the "biggie": Whether or not they will join your company or become a customer. Here are three questions to ask during the close:

1. Do you see why I'm so excited about this?
2. Were you thinking about a few people we could talk to about this?

3. Do you see any reason why we shouldn't go to work right away? *During this part of the close, you should talk 20 percent of the time just to answer questions or overcome objections; the other party should talk 80 percent of the time. The more you talk the less important they will feel. Show them you care by listening.*

After they've answered "yes" to a few soft questions, be bold in asking them to join or become a customer. Say something like, "I'd be honored if you chose to build this business with me. Can we get you started today?"

The close is the most difficult part of the presentation and most people are too afraid to successfully close. Even though it's the most difficult, it's also the most important: You must ask for the close.

Think about it, what will happen to you if your prospect says no? Nothing. You will be exactly where you were before the presentation. However, if they say yes, it's the start of an exciting journey with a new business partner and team member. There's no reason to not ask for the close.

Once you have established a team of your own it is vital that you take leadership in establishing a vision and goals for your team. Do not expect anyone else to take leadership. Be the leader you want to follow. The next chapter will assist you in training yourself and your team how to overcome obstacles.

CHAPTER 6

OVERCOMING OBSTACLES

A hero is an ordinary person who finds the strength to persevere and endure in spite of overwhelming obstacles.

Christopher Reeves

People have fear when it comes to network marketing. As we showed in chapter one the stigma behind network marketing causes many people to become defensive whenever someone talks about the industry. Many people have "tried" different opportunities and failed because they did not have a team willing to help or they did not take the necessary action in order to succeed. When overcoming objections, remember that most objections are based upon fear

You need to answer objections with love, humility, and understanding. Do not argue or insult the person you are showing the business to.

Keep in mind they may not have legitimate reasons for not wanting to do the business, *but they do have legitimate fears.*

Here are the top 10 objections you will face after offering your business opportunity to prospects.

TOP 10 OBJECTIONS:

Objection 1: "I don't have the time."

Possible responses:

- "Great! You're exactly the person I'm looking for. Busy people get things done."
- While smiling say jokingly, "You don't have time to make money?"
- "Aren't you tired of not having time? That's why we do this business—to free our time."
- "I truly appreciate that; I didn't think I had the time either. However, I knew if I didn't change something soon I'd never have time. Do you think this business would be worth your time?"

Objection 2: "I don't have the money."

Possible responses:

- "What could we do to fix that?"
- "If someone paid for you would you do it?" (Note: If they say no it's not a money issue)
- "Aren't you sick of that small amount being a lot of money to you? That's what got me in this business, I was tired of something so minimal being a big deal to me. Let's go make you some money so that never happens again."

- Throw your keys on the table with a smile on your face and say, "Here you go! You can have my car for this amount of money." When they say huh? Respond by saying, "I need you to see the value of this business, not only can you make your money back in virtually no time, you can also earn money for a car that's much better than the one I just offered you."

- This one works only with close friends, "Seriously? You don't have that much money?"

Objection 3: "I've done a business like this before and it didn't work out for me."

Possible responses:

- "I'm so sorry that happened to you. I don't know anything about the other business you were in, but I can tell you that this business is set up for you to succeed. I also know that we as a team are going to build this in a huge way and we take responsibility to ensure you have success as well."

- Jokingly say, "Have you had more than 1 job in your life? When one job didn't work out for you did you say, 'Oh I'll never try another one of those jobs?' No you got another. The same is true in this industry."

Objection 4: "This looks like a pyramid scheme."

Possible responses:

- Ask this question, "Do you know what a pyramid scheme is?" After they answer say one or all of the following:

- "Unfortunately, there have been some pyramid schemes in the world, just like there have been unethical businesses everywhere since the beginning of time. A pyramid scheme indicates that a business is illegal and we would never be a part of an illegal business."

- "A pyramid scheme is when people pay in money and no value is added to any other organization. We add value by acquiring customers for the providers of the different products or services you just saw. In fact, we are some of their best customer gatherers."

Objection 5: "My _____ (Mom, Dad, brother, sister, friend) told me never to get involved in one of these businesses."
Possible responses:

- "I appreciate them taking the time to talk to you about things. With all due respect, is that person willing to pay you the type of money you would like to make? If they are, then you should take their advice. If not, we should get you started right away so you can show them what a beneficial opportunity this can be."

Objection 6: "We already have enough money and don't need anymore."
Possible responses:

- Note: Be very careful with how you answer this objection. "Ok, well let me ask you this. Who could use the money? Is it worth making more money in order to give what you make to others?"

Objection 7: "I need to run it by my spouse."
  Possible responses:

- "Ok, I truly appreciate that. When could we meet again so I can show him or her? You see this business is very important to me and I want to make sure they get all the answers they will look for."

- "On a scale of 1-10 where are you with it? I want to make sure you're above a 6 before you talk with your spouse."

Objection 8: "I need to pray about it."

- Note: Be very careful with how you approach this. "Sounds great! On a scale of 1-10 where do you stand with the opportunity right now?"

Objection 9: "How much money have you made in this business?"

- "According to the direct selling association we're not supposed to share that information. Is that a question you would feel comfortable asking your doctor or lawyer? I need you to see this opportunity with the same respect as another profession."

Objection 10: "I'm not a salesperson."
Possible responses:

- "Have you ever recommended a movie or a restaurant? This industry is based on relationships and recommendations. If you're willing to grow we will teach you how to properly build relationships and recommend products or service."

- "I'm not either. This business just made too much sense. We can make money from these great products/services while recommending them to others."

THE TRUTH ABOUT OBJECTIONS

What seems to be is never what is. Most of the time people come at you with objections what they are really saying is, "I'm afraid." Your job is to help alleviate those fears by using truth. Do not offend or insult the person you are talking to, be empathetic and ask questions to draw out the fears while addressing the fears you already recognize. Sometimes people have good reasons why they do not want to join your opportunity. Be professional and evaluate their reasoning. Getting a "no" is better than getting a "yes" and having someone drop out after a short period of time.

TRY TO GET A YES OR NO

We call people who say maybe "floaters." At any given time you could have up to 100 floaters out there if you don't cut to the chase. It's much easier to ask for a decision than to try to get a hold of people you have already talked to. If someone is floating for good reason they will let you know one way or another. What we suggest you do is follow up one or two times and if a decision is still not made, let the floater go. You do not want uncommitted people on your team.

DEALING WITH REJECTION AND FAILURE

Legendary play writer J.M. Barrie once said, "All of us are failures—at least, all the best of us are." The bottom line is your success will be determined by how you deal with rejection and failures. In his New York Times best seller *Failing Forward*, John Maxwell gives great insight on how we should view negative experiences. He says, "Errors become mistakes when we perceive them and respond to them incorrectly. Mistakes become failures when we continually respond to them incorrectly."

The greatest advice when it comes to failure is to embrace it. We control the way we think, we cannot always control the way we feel, but often times our emotions will follow our thoughts. We teach our team to say these four things over and over again to remind them that failure does not determine who they are.

1. I like myself
2. I love myself
3. I am a business owner
4. I am a professional

We have to condition our minds to separate business and personal things. It can be especially challenging in network marketing because our business is us. Still, if someone says no to the opportunity, that doesn't mean they don't like you or love you. It means they don't like or love the opportunity at that time. Many people join network marketing after watching the success of others.

"NO" DOES NOT MEAN "NEVER"

Again, we can't take rejection personally. Sure, it costs us energy, time, and money to meet with someone who says no. It's valid to feel a bit disappointed. It's what you do with that disappointment that makes the difference. We suggest asking for a referral from the person or asking if you can follow up after a period of time. What is especially effective is what is called "dripping." Make a note to call the person once or twice a month just to talk. Just because they said no doesn't mean you can't be friends or they won't change their mind later on.

We have a person on our team that loves people. This person had a tremendous amount of people tell him no in the first few months of his business. It did not keep this young man from moving forward. After about 8 months of being steady and growing many people who told him no in the beginning started joining his business. He made it a point to keep in touch with all of the people who told him no and eventually over half of his business were people who once said "no."

We must constantly be aware of the voices we listen to. If we spend the majority of our time around negative people, we will think negatively. To consistently overcome objections we have to be intentional about reading and listening to positive things.

Network marketing is a marathon not a sprint; there will be times when you feel like you've hit a wall and you need to stop. At those points is when you must muster up the courage to keep moving forward. Any runner will tell you about their 2nd and 3rd winds. Just when they think they couldn't go another step a burst of energy hits them and another five miles doesn't seem so bad. Perseverance is a long lost art in our culture and it is often the difference between success and failure. Most people would never quit if they realized how close they were to success.

Make a commitment to never, ever quit. Cut out the last part of the failures sentence, "Things got hard...so I quit." Instead make a decision to say "Things were hard...so I kept going." The slight difference in those two sentences makes a monumental difference in everything you put your hands to accomplish. We wish we could tell you everything will go smoothly in your business and no problems will occur. We wish we could tell you all you have to do is believe and magic fairy dust will float you into the heavens.

We will tell you if you believe and choose to do the right things you will fly past the majority of quitters who make excuses instead of realizing their vision. We will tell you if you stick it out you will become the person you never dreamed you could become. We will tell you that if you don't quit you will have the opportunity to affect millions of lives and all the financial benefits will follow. By deciding not to quit when the going gets tough you instantly become different. Never underestimate the power of perseverance.

LEGAL ISSUES IN NETWORK MARKETING

One thing many direct selling owners have said over and over again is this will never be a perfect industry. At the same time they have said they will do their best to be a great industry. Unfortunately legal issues arise in business regardless of the industry, product, or location. Companies like Wal-mart, McDonalds, and General Electric all have had numerous lawsuits against them right. Some cases they have lost. However, they continue to move forward. Why? Legal matters are a part of the imperfect world of business.

One thing we do not want to do is downplay the legal issues that have taken place. What we want is to be fair and logical.

Logically we understand that people sue company's everyday in order to line their pockets without having to work. For some, suing a company is the same as buying a lottery ticket. Is this true in all cases? No. But logically we know people are people and we need to keep that in mind when evaluating issues.

Also, we must understand that not all people do what they are supposed to do. They join their company with the belief that if they sit long enough a golden egg will hatch treasures at their feet.

Unfortunately that is not the case and it takes a lot of work to make the type of money we all desire. However, people who believe they should have a golden egg without having to work sometimes sue based upon that belief.

Most all successful companies face lawsuits at some point in their lifecycle. Companies like Wal-mart, McDonalds and General Electric have all face their share of lawsuits and the negative press that accompanies them. Unfortunately, resistance is a part of doing business.

Obstacles will occur to keep you from fulfilling your vision. How you deal with those obstacles will determine your success as a network marketer. Develop perseverance and decide to get a little better every day and you will get to where you want to go.

CHAPTER 7

BUILDING SUCCESS

Always bear in mind that your own resolution to succeed is more important than any other.

Abraham Lincoln

No successful person ever achieves success by accident. They have a plan, they have discipline and they have character. Before we discuss the different aspects of planning, discipline and character we need to define success. Success is a science; many people have their own hypothesis, but it has a level of relativity. Larry Polanda says "Success is the realization of a worthwhile dream." David Brinkley said, "A successful man is one who can lay a firm foundation from the bricks others have thrown at him."

One of the most famous definitions of success comes from Winston Churchill, "Success consists of going from failure to failure without any loss of enthusiasm."

Success can be elusive and does not last very long in certain areas. We view successful people as those who maintained at least a modicum of success in their lives or as people who are currently enjoying success. During their reign at the top of the pop charts in 1997, British band Chumbawamba made huge splashes with their song "Tubthumping." Any mainstream radio listener would have considered the band successful during the late 90's. However, a few years after the songs fame died down fewer and fewer people considered the band a mainstream success. Why?

Success is evaluated by the whole body of work and not periods of time. This is a very important point to remember as you begin to see success in your business. If you're going to be successful, you can't allow success to slow you down. It's easy to become comfortable when you reach a pinnacle in your lives so planning your future is so important.

PLANNING

We train our students and team members to make 5, 10, and 20-year vision and mission statements and daily, weekly and monthly action plans. G.K. Chesterton once said, "Reading makes a learned man, writing makes a precise man." Writing your vision and mission statement and action plans will help you become precise and give you a defined standard of production. Remember, if you have nothing to aim at, you'll hit precisely that. Complete the following and place these where you will see them every day.

VISION STATEMENTS

5, 10 and 20-year vision statements – Describe where you see yourself in this time period. Describe what occupation you will have, where you see your spouse, children, and other family members. Describe where you will be working and whatever else you will have accomplished by this time. Be detailed.

Mission statements (4 total)
Your mission statement articulates your role and what your purpose is. It should also say what you want to be. Develop mission statements for the following areas of your life:

- family
- business
- social
- personal

Your mission statement should be written in light of your vision statement. This is the mission you are on to carry out your vision for areas of your life. Describe what character traits you will implement in order to carry your mission out. Be detailed.

DAILY AND WEEKLY ACTION PLAN

Create a daily and weekly schedule that will emanate your mission and vision statements. What things can you plan consistently that will keep you moving towards your mission and vision statements?

Use the following examples:

Monday

9:30 a.m. -10 a.m. – Read "Verbal Advantage." This book will help increase my vocabulary and help me become an effective communicator.

Thursday

6 p.m.-6:25 p.m. – I will go for a walk. This will help me become healthier and increase my stamina and my self-confidence.

Once you've completed these steps, print them out and put them in a place where you'll see them often. These goals will become habits and thinking processes. Your discipline will determine if you'll achieve these goals.

DISCIPLINE

Reaching your goals won't happen by accident; seeing your goals on paper will matter only if you take action steps to achieve them. Leadership has two faces—transformational and transactional. Transformation happened the first time you saw your business opportunity and you realized it could help you reach your dreams. Transaction happened when you paid to own your franchise and decided to sell the products and services and build you team. If you want to be a successful person you must have a consistent combination of both transformational and transactional.

Discipline and consistency are old friends. A survey was given at Newlife Technical Institute asking students what was their most valued character trait. Number one was consistency.

People appreciate and follow people they can count on. Consistency is power. Let's think about this for a moment: When you tell someone you are going to do something and you follow through, you essentially told that person two things.

One, I care about you and two, I am consistent and you can trust my word. Think about the power in that! When someone cancels appointments at the last minute or doesn't show up, they are telling the person the opposite of those two things. Who would you rather do business with?

We must be disciplined in being consistent. When you are consistent people will take you seriously and you will earn respect for your organization. If you say you will deliver something. Deliver it. When you say you are going to be somewhere. Be there. When you commit to your team; stay committed through tough times. In an interview with *Success Magazine*, Marshall Goldsmith said, "Success is finding what works, and pressing the 'REPEAT' button." Find what works in your business and do it over and over again while encouraging those on your team to do the same. As you are disciplined in consistency, you will see results.

DISCIPLINE: ONE STEP AT A TIME

Recently, we had a person on our team who was struggling with discipline. We asked this person to pick one thing they would like to be better at--just one. They decided to wake up earlier.

We helped them pick a time they could wake up consistently at least five days a week. We agreed 6 a.m. was a good time for them. We asked them to start by waking up at that time every single day for a week and not add anything to it. After a week that person came back and reported they woke up every day the past week at 6 a.m. and to fill their time they started reading a book we recommended to them.

After a month the person read the entire book and was starting to see a great difference in their thinking. The next month they added a new discipline, so forth and so on. This person is now helping train groups of people in network marketing. All of this started by changing one discipline at a time.

There is a misconception in our culture that if results don't happen quickly it must not be worth it. In fact, the opposite is true. All things worth having are worth the wait and worth working hard for. Think what could happen in your life if you added one positive discipline per month. You would have 12 new disciplines per year. What if you added two positive disciplines per month? Imagine the possibilities.

DEALING WITH BAD HABITS

We all have them; we all love and hate them at the same time. Bad habits are like bad pennies; they always show up at the worst times. Dealing with bad habits is similar to adding good habits; you must do it one step at a time. Do not try to change all your habits at once. It won't happen for very long. The best way to defeat bad habits is to change them one at a time. Pick one, any one and exchange it with a positive habit. Be intentional about it. Let's say you want to stop listening to negative news. To fill your time, get motivational or encouraging CDs to listen to in your car as you drive to work. If you want to stop eating that extra portion at dinner, drink more water instead. The list could go on and on, but make sure you are always taking action steps to defeat the negative behaviors in your life.

The best part about overcoming bad habits is the results. Although you focus on one habit at a time, you almost never change one at a time. Think about it, let's say you are making an effort to be kinder to people. Kindness is a great goal, but is not alone. Generosity, friendliness, compassion, and grace all come with kindness, so you've essentially added four new habits because you focused on being more kind. We will live up to our goals, visions, and values. This is why it is so important that we are intentional about iterating and reiterating them, looking at them daily, and having a person to hold us accountable.

Discipline isn't something nice to have or not have. It is one of the most important aspects of your business. Start disciplining yourself. Let discipline and consistency become old friends of yours.

CHAPTER 8

BUILDING A NEW COMFORT ZONE

Comfort and prosperity have never enriched the world as much as

adversity has.

Billy Graham

Pastor Mike Ross once said, "People achieve to their level of comfort. They don't care if they have the most money or win the race; they just want to be comfortable." Let's take a story from the Bible. After 400 years in captivity, God used Moses to free the Hebrew people from slavery. While leaving Egypt God performed many miracles, the most famous being the parting of the Red Sea, He also provided manna, water, and showed Himself in the form of a pillar of cloud by day and fire by night.

After all of this the Hebrews still would not follow His instructions to go into the Promised Land. Instead, they wanted to go back to Egypt where they were enslaved.

It is easy to look at this story and talk about how foolish these people were. Jim Rohn used to say "The Bible is a great guide for telling us what to do and what not to do." The story of the Hebrews is not far from many network marketers or network marketing teams. The Hebrews were afraid of the people in Canaan. We are afraid we will be told no.

The Hebrews did not trust their leaders. We don't trust our leaders. The Hebrews complained because they were "comfortable" in Egypt and although in slavery, they knew where their meals were coming from. We complain in network marketing because it is hard sometimes and we are comfortable working nine to five building someone else's kingdom just like the Hebrews built for the Egyptians.

What are we afraid of? Why did we give up on the dreams we had when we were kids? Do we really sacrifice all of those great things for comfort? As much as it pains us to admit the answer is yes. It is uncomfortable to call someone and ask for an appointment. It is uncomfortable to commit to meetings every week. It is uncomfortable to train someone who may not get all the concepts at first.

So what? Is being uncomfortable for short periods of time worth being in bondage to money? Is it worth letting our dreams fade in the sunset? Is it worth giving up on an opportunity to use your God-given talents and abilities for all their worth?

Only you can answer the questions above. We have given you the tools to achieve your dreams in this industry. It is now up to you. We want more than anything to see you achieve your God-given potential, but you have to be willing to step out of your comfort zone consistently to get there. Do not choose comfort over your dreams. Do not allow them to fade or have others live them for you. Become the best you possible; we only have one shot, one opportunity at this life. Let it be a life that changes and affects others. You have it in you to be great. Choose a new comfort zone; a comfort zone that is comfortable with being uncomfortable.

We look forward to seeing you reach the top.

APPENDIX A
30 Days to Success
A Checklist for the First Month in Your Business

First 24 hours

☐ Become familiar with the products or services your company offers

✓ Write down or highlight the top 3 you feel you will have the easiest time marketing

✓ Write down 3 highlights of each of the three.

☐ Create your **WHY** list

✓ Write "Why" at the top of the paper, include 3-5 reasons why you are doing this business (ex. Become your own boss, build generational wealth for your family etc.)

✓ Place your "Why" list in a place where you will see it daily (ex. Refrigerator, mirror, bathroom, etc)

☐ Write a customer list

✓ Include yourself

✓ Include at least 3 people you believe would sign up for products/services.

✓ This list is for customers, not prospective business partners—*however, don't assume too much*—show prospective customers the business as well

☐ Write a partner list

✓ Include people who do you believe would like to make money bills they already pay

✓ Create a 3 Tier system for potential partners

- Tier 1 – People who are outgoing, have money, and connections

- Tier 2 – People who have 2 of the above

- Tier 3 – People who have 1 of the above

First 7 days
☐ Gather 5 customers

✓ These points are in addition to what you start your business with

✓ Listen to training manual CD

☐ Get with your sponsor and make 5-10 appointments with potential customers and partners

☐ Do a mock presentation with your sponsor

☐ Listen to training CD's and watch training DVD's

☐ Review material and understand compensation plan

First 14 days
☐ Make 10-15 appointments to meet with potential customers and partners

☐ Watch training CD's and watch training DVD's

☐ Gather another outside customer

☐ Review material

✓ Be able to explain compensation plan

✓ Understand how to sign-up customers and partners in the system

☐ Attend weekly business meeting and training session.

First 21 days
☐ Learn how to teach new representatives to gather their customers

☐ Make 5-10 appointments

☐ Listen to training CD's and watch training DVD

☐ Review pertinent material and the compensation plan with your

☐ Sit down with sponsor, do mock presentation and explain business model

First 30 days
☐ Make 5 appointments

☐ Help your sponsor make 10-15 appointments for potential customers and business partners

☐ Listen to training CD's and watch training DVD's

☐ Gather 2 more personal customers

☐ Review the presentation, compensation plan, and product/services with your sponsor

☐ Make sure you can do the business presentation on your own (if needed)

What if I do not complete this checklist within 30 days?
No worries! Simply continue focusing on the checklist and finish it as you can. If you do this in 60, 90, or even 6 months it will still be effective. However, the key to effective team building is to keep pace with others who follow the process.

Can I just gather customers and not business partners?
Yes! In many companies you can promote by gathering customers. Remember we are paid through the customers gathered by each partner and not through signing up business partners. However, the beauty of this business model is we can create a team of customer gatherers (or partners) that can gather that amount of customers in 1/10 of the time it would take you to personally gather those customers. Leveraging your time is the key.

How much time do I need to complete the 30 day checklist?
Typically the checklist will require each representative 6 to 12 hours per month. This is focused time. It is important to remember that this is a business and you must spend focused time on your business daily. Whether it is 15 minutes or 10 hours, you must do something with your business every single day. Neglect is the silent killer of many network marketing businesses.

NOTES

ENDNOTES

Oakley, E. & Krug, D. (1991). *Enlightened leadership: Getting to the heart of Change.* New York: Simon & Schuster.

Schein, E. H. (2004). *Organizational culture and leadership.* (3rd Ed.). San Francisco: Jossey-Bass Publishers.

Kouzes, J. & Posner B. (2003). *Encouraging the Heart: A Leaders guide to rewarding and recognizing others.* San Francisco: Jossey-Bass Publishers.

Myers, D.G. (2004). *Psychology Seventh Edition in Modules.* (7th Ed.). New York: Worth Publishers.

Stanley, A. (1999). *Visioneering: God's blueprint for developing and maintaining vision.* Colorado Springs: Multnoma Publishers.

Batterson, M. (2006). *In a Pit with a Lion on a Snowy Day.* Colorado Springs, CO: Multnoma Publishers.

Maxwell, J. (2000). *Failing Forward: Turning mistakes into stepping stones for success.* Nashville: Thomas Nelson, Inc.

Matteson, M. (2006). *Freedom from Fear Forever.* Mechanicsburg, PA: Executive Books.

Carnegie, Dale (1936). *How to Win Friends and Influence People.* New York, NY. Simon &Shuster Inc.

Hill, A. (2008). *Just Business: Christian Ethics in the Marketplace.* (2nd Ed.) Downers Grove, IL: InterVarsity Press.

Covey, S. (1994). *First Things First.* New York: Free Press.

Thomas, K. W. (2002). *Intrinsic Motivation at Work: Building Energy and Commitment.* San Francisco: Berrett-Koehler Publishers, Inc.

Pink, M.Q. (2000). *Selling Among Wolves without joining the pack.* Gainesville, FL: Bridge-Logos.

Hardy, D. (2010). *The Compound Effect: Multiplying your success, one simple step at a time.* Dallas: Success Books.

Thomas, L. (2011). *Online Marketing*. McGraw-Hill.

Rohm, R.A. (1999). *Positive Personality Profiles: "D-I-S-C-OVER" Personality insights to understand Yourself...and others!*. (10th Ed.) Atlanta, GA: Personality Insights, Inc.

Rubino, J. (2006). *The Ultimate Guide to Network Marketing: 37 Top income-earners share their most preciously guarded secrets to building extreme wealth*. Hoboken, NJ: John Wiley & Sons, Inc.

Barrett, D.J. (2008). *Leadership communication* (2nd ed.). Boston: McGraw-Hill Irwin.

The NIV Student Bible, Revised. (2002). Grand Rapids, Michigan: Zondervan.

Harrison, E.F. (1999). *The managerial decision-making process*. (5th ed.) Boston: Houghton Mifflin.

Anderson, Arthur. (1992). *The Anderson 7-Step Model*. Geneva College 01.31.08

Wilkens, S. (1995). *Beyond bumper sticker ethics: An introduction to theories of right & wrong*. Downers Grove, Il: InterVarsity Press.

Denning, S. (2004). Telling tales. *Harvard Business Review*, 82(5), 1-7.

Allen, From Scott. "The Real Problem with Network Marketing and Multi-Level Marketing (MLM)." *Entrepreneurs - Starting and Running Your Own Business*. Web. 26 Apr. 2010. <http://entrepreneurs.about.com/cs/multilevelmktg/a/problemwithmlm.htm>.

Rocavert, Troy. "History of Network Marketing – FREE Tutorial on MLM." *Network Marketing Business School - Everything You Need to Know about MLM*. 2008. Web. 26 Apr. 2010. <http://www.network-marketing-business-school.com/history-of-network-marketing.html>.

Rubino, Joe. *The Ultimate Guide to Network Marketing: 37 Top Network Marketing Income-earners Share Their Most Preciously Guarded Secrets to Building Extreme Wealth*. Hoboken, N.J.: John Wiley & Sons, 2006. Print.

Stewart, Greg. "MLM Truth and History." *Affordable Proven Worldwide MLM Software*. 2010. Web. 26 Apr. 2010. <http://www.internetnextstep.com/mlmsecret.htm>.

Taylor, Jon. "Key Legal Issues." *Truth on MLM or Network Marketing*. 2010. Web. 26 Apr. 2010. <http://www.mlm-thetruth.com/content/KeyLegalIssues>.

ABOUT THE AUTHORS

Michael Ross, Co-founder of Mainstream Life Solutions, is a visioneer from Ohio who has a heart to see others live their dreams and reach their maximum potential. He's driven by a strong conviction that each individual was created to be extraordinary and do extraordinary things.

After stepping out of a steady job in corporate America, Michael pursued his calling: teaching and training others to develop into fulfilled and influential individuals.

Michael is a successful business owner and entrepreneur. He has a master's degree in Organizational Leadership from Geneva College. He is a United States Navy veteran and has served in Afghanistan, Iraq, South Korea, Japan and several other places around the globe. Michael's experience in the Navy has contributed to his ability to see beyond the "small town" mentality and make an impact at the global level.

Michael is an expert in character training and is skilled in teaching financial independence. He, his wife Brittany and their son, Zaiden, reside in Ohio. They are active in their church and collaborate in speaking engagements across the region.

David Baker, Co-founder of Mainstream Life Solutions, has trained and coached hundreds of people in the United States, Canada and Europe in the art of selling and branding business. He has also founded numerous businesses and has taught audiences how to become champions in business and life.

David started his career in marketing and sales. He became a top sales volume producer for a Fortune 500 Company and later became a corporate Sales & Marketing director for a Pittsburgh based company. He was instrumental in building a sales force that produced over 75 million dollars per year. In 1995 David gave up the 9 to 5 lifestyle and set out to pursue his dreams. David's passion for research and study in the field of motivational psychology and business led him into the network marketing, affiliate marketing, real estate investing, social entrepreneurship, and business education.

David is skilled in transferring his passion of business and motivational psychology to his students. He specializes in teaching people how to achieve their dreams. He has conducted seminars, workshops and speeches across the United States, Canada, and Europe.

His ability to combine the theoretical with the practical is powerful, direct, and enlightening. His work is a reflection of his commitment to motivating people to achieve the greatness God has planned for them.

David was educated at Kent State and Michigan State Universities in Business Management and Mechanical Engineering. He and his wife Roberta reside in Eastern Ohio where they enjoy the company of their 8 children and 5 grandchildren.